CALENDARS

BOOKS BY ANNIE FINCH

Books of Poetry

The Encyclopedia of Scotland (1982)
Catching the Mermother (chapbook, 1996)
Eve (1997)
Season Poems (chapbook, 2001)
Calendars (2003)

Books About Poetry

The Ghost of Meter: Culture and Prosody in American Free Verse (1993)

As Editor

A Formal Feeling Comes (1994)
After New Formalism (1999)
Perspectives on Carolyn Kizer (co-editor with Johanna Keller and Candace McClelland, 2001)
An Exaltation of Forms (co-editor with Kathrine Varnes, 2002)

CALENDARS

Annie Finch

T P

TUPELO PRESS
Dorset, Vermont

No woman should be shamefaced in attempting to give back to the world,
through her work, a portion of its lost heart.

—Louise Bogan

Form is the wave, emptiness the water.

—Thich Nhat Hanh

For my mother

Margaret Rockwell Finch

Acknowledgments

Grateful acknowledgment is given to the following journals, books, and anthologies where poems in this manuscript have previously appeared, often in different or very different versions.

Ablemuse.com: "Chain of Women," "A Wedding on Earth," "Final Autumn," "Two Bodies," "A Carol for Carolyn," "Paravaledellentine"; *American Voice:* "Ghazal for a Poetess"; *Alaska Quarterly Review:* "Winter Solstice," "The Coming Mirrors"; *Beloit Poetry Journal:* "The Menstrual Hut," "Iowa Barn," "Over Dark Arches"; *Carolyn Kizer: Perspectives:* "A Carol for Carolyn"; *Connecticut Review:* "Valentine for Hands," "Caribou Kitchen," "Moon"; *Drunken Boat:* "Belly," "Churching"; *Eclectic Literary Forum:* "Wild Yeasts"; *Field:* "Blue Willows"; *Go 2:* "Two Bodies," "The Coming Mirrors"; *Hudson Review:* "Lamia to Lycius"; *Lyric (CityLights):* "Summer Solstice"; *Many Mountains Moving:* "Hostage Wildflowers"; *Marlboro Review:* "Name," "Boothbay Harbor"; *Michigan Quarterly Review:* "Iowa Barn," "Dance for the Inland Sea"; *Notre Dame Review:* "A Letter for Emily Dickinson," "Faces With Poulenc"; *Paris Review:* "For Vivienne Eliot"; *Partisan Review:* "Landing Under Water, I See Roots"; *Prairie Schooner:* "Chain of Women," "Desire for Quiet," "Earth Goddess and Sky God," "Forest Falling," "Paravaledellentine," "A Seed for Spring Equinox"; *Prayers to Protest:* "Winter Solstice"; *Ravishing DisUnities: Real Ghazals in English:* "Ghazal for a Poetess"; *Salt:* "Interpenetrate," "Paravaledellentine"; *Schuykill Valley Journal:* "Elegy for My Father," "A Carol for Carolyn"; *Simone Weil and the Intellect of Grace:* "Elegy for My Father"; *Daughters and Sons to Fathers:* "Elegy for My Father"; *Contemporary Poets on Emily Dickinson:* "Letter for Emily Dickinson"; *Wallace Stevens Journal:* "The Woman on the Beach"; *Whirligig:* "Butterfly Lullaby"; *Words for Images (Yale University Art Gallery):* "Conversation"; *Yale Lit:* "The August Porch"; *Yale Review:* "The Intellect of Woman"

"Imbolc," "A Seed for Spring Equinox," "Summer Solstice," "Lammas Chant," and "Winter Solstice" are included in the chapbook *Season Poems* (Calliope Press, 2002). Versions of "Two Bodies," "Chain of Women," "Butterfly Lullaby," "Over Dark Arches," and "The Coming Mirrors" were set to music as part of "Cantata for My Daughter," written for Althea, with music composed by Stefania de Kennessey, performed by the New York Women's Choir. "Landing Under Water, I See Roots" was recorded on C.D. as part of the composition "In Memoriam" with music by Stefania De Kennessey. "Landing Under Water," "Boothbay Harbor," and "The Woman on the Beach" were part of the poetry puppet performance "Landing Under Water: A Mermaid's Tale," with puppets and scenery by Lisa Siders-Kenney, directed by Beth Franks.

"Landing Under Water, I See Roots" is dedicated to Rita Dove's *The Darker Face of the Earth.* "Chain of Women" is dedicated to Adrienne Rich's *Of Woman Born.* "Belly" is dedicated to Marie Borroff. "Faces With Poulenc" is dedicated to Julie, and to Harvey Hess. "A Wedding on Earth" is for Roy and Susie, with love. Thanks to Billy Collins for inventing the paradelle. My warm gratitude to Agha Shahid Ali, John Drury, Beth Franks, Johanna Keller, Maxine Kumin, Phillis Levin, Bill Mitten, Pat Mora, A.E. Stallings, and Robert Ward for helpful comments and insights. Deepest thanks to Lisa Siders-Kenney, Lisa Storie, and to the wom-po listserv for profound encouragement over the long haul. I am grateful to sensitive reader Lyn Chase, talented manuscript editor Bob Clawson, perpetual inspiration Maggie Finch, honest Judith Kitchen, and friend-of-the-freethinking Carolyn Kizer for frank and wide-ranging help with the manuscript. My gratitude to Glen Brand (who in every astute and generous way imaginable has helped this book to exist), and to Julian and Althea (for their inspiring love and tireless example), and to Jeffrey Levine of Tupelo Press (who brought this version of the book out from the underworld), is awed, delighted and neverending.

Grateful acknowledgement to John Hughes, the College of Arts and Sciences, Keith Tuma, the Department of English, Carol Willeke and the Center for the Advancement of Scholarship and Teaching, all of the Miami University in Oxford, Ohio for their generous support of a cloth edition.

Contents

Epithalamium

Two Bodies

Earth Goddess and Sky God

Landing Under Water

Landing Under Water, I See Roots

All the things we hide in water
hoping we won't see them go—
(forests growing under water
press against the ones we know)—

and they might have gone on growing
and they might now breathe above
everything I speak of sowing
(everything I try to love).

Moon

Then are you the dense everywhere that moves,
the dark matter they haven't yet walked through?

(No, I'm not. I'm just the shining sun,
sometimes covered up by the darkness).

But in your beauty—yes, I know you see—
There is no covering, no constant light.

The Menstrual Hut

How can I listen to the moon?
Your blood will listen, like a charm.

I knew a way to feel the sun
as if a statue felt warm eyes.
Even with ruins on the moon,
your blood will listen, every time.

Now I am the one with eyes.
Your blood can listen, every time.

Letter For Emily Dickinson

When I cut words you never may have said
into fresh patterns, pierced in place with pins,
ready to hold them down with my own thread,
they change and twist sometimes, their color spins
loose, and your spider generosity
lends them from language that will never be
free of you after all. My sampler reads,
"called back." It says, "she scribbled out these screeds."
It calls, "she left this trace, and now we start"—
in stitched directions that follow the leads
I take from you, as you take me apart.

You wrote some of your lines while baking bread,
propping a sheet of paper by the bins
of salt and flour, so if your kneading led
to words, you'd tether them as if in thin
black loops on paper. When they sang to be free,
you captured those quick birds relentlessly
and kept a slow, sure mercy in your deeds,
leaving them room to peck and hunt their seeds
in the white cages your vast iron art
had made by moving books, and lives, and creeds.
I take from you as you take me apart.

To Vivienne Eliot

Your gray dress stings in the canopied dawn

(Cassandra has hair that is twisted, and curls)

your eyes aren't closed and your hair is wild

(she is gaunt, very strong, as loud as a gong)

your gray dress stings, and the man is gone

(going morning, and there is nothing she ignores)

your eyes aren't closed, your hair is wild

(If I watch her face curl, burned with anger, the pearl)

your gray dress stings, in the canopied dawn

(that has coated the sand will dissolve in my hand)

Watching the Oregon Whale

A hard gray wave, her fin, walks out on the water
that thickens to open and then parts open, around her.

Measured by her delved water, I follow her fill
into and out of green light in the depth she has spun

through the twenty-six fathoms of her silent orison,
then sink with her till she rises, lulled with the krill.

Beads of salt spray stop me, like metal crying.
Her cupped face breathes its spouts, like a jewel-wet prong.

In a cormorant's barnacle path, I trail her, spun
down through my life in the making of her difference,

fixing my mouth, with the offerings of silence,
on her dark whale-road where all green partings run,

where ocean's hidden bodies twist fathoms around her,
making her green-fed hunger grow fertile as water.

_____ Name

Winter Solstice Chant

December 22

Vines, leaves, roots of darkness, growing,
now you are uncurled and cover our eyes
with the edge of winter sky
leaning over us in icy stars.
Vines, leaves, roots of darkness, growing,
come with your seasons, your fullness, your end.

Blue Willow

Once days blew in a pattern, when blue willows
bent where they blew, and bowls filled with birds
and plates arched out from them. Days blew across cups,
and covered the stories on saucers, and then the week came.

It's morning. Day rises above me,
and my own house, and the door, the tea in the cup
that you sip from, the blue willow china,
till more sun leans over the backs of the chairs—

Name

Brown-gold with bronze water, broken in blossom,
they shake as you shine over swans, your wedged bodies
pushing the sky towards the monumented island
where long generations of geese flew before you.

Long generations of geese flew before you,
sang out, and melted over the graves.
Won't long cries of feathers pile a moment
close on another? Isn't there one name?

Close on another, isn't there one name?
Mourning I ask you, mourning I ask you.
So went the questions the geese did not answer:
is this voice a music you mourn with, each time?

Is this voice a music you mourn with, each time?
When questions had asked me, I moved in their bodies
and followed the light on the movement of swans,

and followed the movement of light on the swans.

Elegy For My Father

HLF, August 8, 1918 – August 22, 1997

"Bequeath us to no earthly shore until
Is answered in the vortex of our grave
The seal's wide spindrift gaze towards paradise."
—Hart Crane, "Voyages"

"If a lion could talk, we couldn't understand it"
—Ludwig Wittgenstein

Under the ocean that stretches out wordlessly
past the long edge of the last human shore,
there are deep windows the waves haven't opened,
where night is reflected through decades of glass.
There is the nursery, there is the nanny,
there are my father's unreachable eyes
turned towards the window. Is the child uneasy?
His is the death that is circling the stars.

In the deep room where candles burn soundlessly
and peace pours at last through the cells of our bodies,
three of us are watching, one of us is staring
with the wide gaze of a wild, wave-fed seal.
Incense and sage speak in smoke loud as waves,
and crickets sing sand towards the edge of the hourglass.
We wait outside time, while night collects courage
around us. The vigil is wordless. And you

watch the longest, move the farthest, besieged by your breath,
pulling into your body. You stare towards your death,
head arched on the pillow, your left fingers curled.
Your mouth sucking gently, unmoved by these hours
and their vigil of salt spray, you show us how far
you are going, and how long the long minutes are,
while spiralling night watches over the room
and takes you, until you watch us in turn.

Lions speak their own language. You are still breathing.
Here is release. Here is your pillow,
cool like a handkerchief pressed in a pocket.
Here is your white tousled long growing hair.
Here is a kiss on your temple to hold you
safe through your solitude's long steady war;
here, you can go. We will stay with you,
keeping the silence we all came here for.

Night, take his left hand, turning the pages.
Spin with the windows and doors that he mended.
Spin with his answers, patient, impatient.
Spin with his dry independence, his arms
warmed by the needs of his family, his hands
flying under the wide, carved gold ring, and the pages
flying so his thought could fly. His breath slows,
lending its edges out to the night.

Here is his open mouth. Silence is here
like one more new question that he will not answer.
A leaf is his temple. The dark is the prayer.
He has given his body; his hand lies above
the sheets in a symbol of wholeness, a curve
of thumb and forefinger, ringed with wide gold,
and the instant that empties his breath is a flame
faced with a sudden cathedral's new stone.

Final Autumn

Maple leaves turn black in the courtyard.
Light drives lower and one bluejay crams
our cold memories out past the sun,

each time your traces come past the shadows
and visit under my looking-glass fingers
that lift and block out the sun.

Come—I'll trace you one final autumn,
and you can trace your last homecoming
into the snow or the sun.

Mowing

Easing the land into one long-plotted scene,
we stroke grass into piles with the rake.
Earth's face goes quiet, moved to a docile green
tinge blushed for other eyes, not for our sake.
Harrow the lawn, pack leaves of grass to loam,
flatten the seed-tall walls that would twist and sigh
around us, carve down the rooted caves that foam
with causeless silence, kill the lace-long sky.
Why harvest a grain whose worth is to remain
and ignore the seeds, leaving the yield unkept,
trudging lost kernels to such empty gain?
Won't we have reaped until we've stopped and swept
all the harvest away? Must we stand to see
our plain land lie with hands open, and empty?

Forest-Falling

To my unborn

Under the leaves where you'd be lying,
life makes woods of Tennessee
where leaves and loam grow down, drying
brown from chlorophyll and tree.
Needles that loosen, where you'd be,
range to the ground or graze down
the tunneled heights so quietly
they have not gathered. On the ground,
under the needles where I would like you to break
         and drown,

tunnels fill the earth like foam,
the sentried, calm land breaks down,
and fungi blacken into loam.
Would seas of insects wash the brown
and buttressed skies with catacombs?
Would leaves the trees gave up to spin
through the teeth of their waiting, branching comb
weave you back again? You would begin
to rot into those trees whose forest we have been,

where root hair cells would take you in,
where I'd thread through if I could break
out from the trees that forest in
my branch with leaves, where I would
make ground for the earth if I could,
take sounds of all your unheard trying
down with me to fall, and break,
ranging the tunnels that are only dying,
circling so slowly, circling them, and crying.

Without A Bird

This is a dawn
without a sun

(that has no birds)

This is a dawn
that will not part

(that will not sing)

Night has no birds
that will not sing

(out of this cold)

This is a dawn
This is a dawn

(that is not spring)

Boothbay Harbor

When ocean
pulls towards ocean,
leaving seaweed
on the rocks,

it will dry
to curl outward
with the blossom
of the salt.

Caribou Kitchen

Most things have vanished
while we were talking
(the dents in a pitcher
gleam by the gas lamp),
but nothing is lost
(cups in far corners).
Arms still lean
over the table
(shadows on the oilcloth).

Calendars

Imbolc Chant

February 2

From the east she has gathered like wishes.
She has woven a night into dawn.
We are quickening ivy. We grow
where her warmth melts out over the ice.

Now spiral south bends into flame
to push the morning into doors.
The light swings wide, green with the pulse
of seasons, and we let her in

          We are quickening ivy. We grow

The light swings wide, green with the pulse

          till the west is rocked by darkness
          pulled from where her fire rises.
          Shortened time's reflecting water
          rakes her through the thickened cold.

Then hands cover north smooth with emptiness,
stinging the mill of night's hours.
Wait with me. See, she comes circling
over the listening snow to us.

          Shortened time's reflecting water

      Wait with me. See, she comes circling

Calendars

A poem in chants for four voices:

Demeter

Chorus

Persephone

Hades

In the winding
of the vine
our voices stretch
from us and twine—

No, going into the waiting places
is not easy. Flowers fade there.

around the year's
fermented wine—

Mostly, it's surrender of wanting,
or the fear that a flame will be dampened—

or that everything warm will come rushing
over me with reproach—or that endless

needles could be ranged in the tunnel—
or that my bare feet would be slippery—

Yellow. Fall roars
down to the ground,
loud, in the leafy sun that pours
liquid through doors.
Yellow, the leaves go down

or that once I'm down in that darkness
someone outside will block off the entrance,

Touches of gold stipple the branches,
promising weeks of time—

Thread With Me

My lover, when you riddle with me—

reddening slowly, then suddenly free,
turned like a key

Oh! the falling flowers have caught me
by dipping yellow, purple towards the hunger—

—the hard, the intricate dark
(I hear the notes of your words
ring for me cool as the birds,

my lover—

through the long year's
fermenting wine

her thin stems turning, held to be—lost—

my lover, when you thread with me

Now you are uncurled and cover our eyes
with the edge of winter sky,
leaning over us in icy stars

through this night-shot
night-shot dark

is never easy.

Flowers fade here.

Voices pull me on through the cavern
from the new season. Her voice old, silent—

our hands, our breasts, our curves
curl through our hands and ravel—

On damp limestone, a violet curling—

my lover, when you riddle with me
the hard, the intricate dark.

Rack me with courage, spring,
come kill me, flowers;

if we are shadows, come;

make me our shadows

as I reach for flowers.

Interpenetrate

A Seed for Spring Equinox

March 21

...till I feel the earth around the place my head has lain
under winter's touch, and it crumbles. Slanted weight of clouds.
Reaching with my head and shoulders past the open crust

dried by spring wind. Sun. Tucking through the ground
that has grown its cold inside me, made its waiting into food.
Now I watch the watching dark my light's long-growing dark makes known.

Interpenetrate

Like the bleached fibers and their haunted ink,
interpenetrate each others' solitudes,

not penetrating, not dissolving; stay
rolled with the single patterns of the days,

linking through pages to burn with speaking lace
and thread to bodies, evenly alive.

The Woman on the Beach
for Wallace Stevens

She could cliff and order waves, if they were climb-
ing up to reach her touch, or curling in
with drowning, freezing, fingers… She hears

the phantoms tooling over shale, their long
unrooting waverings singing the air
into her hands. Then, as she plants and pours,
learning her music, with no difference how

she seeds them out, or harvests in, or racks
the dark with her questioning, she pulls the caves
from sleep with her answering chant and noticing shore.
The waves won't hear her now; she won't feed them;

and it won't matter how she pulls them in,
gathers their green in seedlings weighted all
spiralling through, to make her bounded dream.

33

Chain Of Women

These are the seasons Persephone promised
as she turned on her heel—
the ones that darken, till green no longer
bandages what I feel.

Now touches of gold stipple the branches,
promising weeks of time
to fade through, finding the footprints
she left as she turned to climb.

A Carol For Carolyn

"It is easy to be a poet,
brim with transparent water."

—Carolyn Kizer, "In the First Stanza"

I dreamed of a poet who gave me a whale
that shadowed clear pools through the kelp-making shade.
When beached sea-foam dried on the rocks, it would sail
down currents that gathered to pool and cascade
with turbulent order.
She brims with transparent water,
as mother and poet and daughter.

The surface is broken and arching and full,
impelled by the passions of nation and woman.
The waves build and fall; the deep currents pull
toward rocky pools cupping the salt of the human.
The ocean she's authored
brims, with transparent water,
for poet and mother and daughter.

Faces With Poulenc

Here in waiting's shuddered
sway, which makes a hand
a mouth, a song a breath,

under a ceiling turned
curving by music, pour
tremors bold as hills, Poulenc.

Turn down your light heads
as if a breath could last,
photographs and flowers—

until the heavy, hunting
oboe focusses
its only simple face

and the patterning tip
we search with touches charmed
aches and passes on.

Ghazal For A Poetess

Many the nights that have passed,
But I remember
The river of pearls at Fez
And Seomar whom I loved.

— Laurence Hope, 1903

The corners of the frontispiece yellow from their darker edges.
Aching eyes lift in tremolo from their darker edges.

Moon lit your blood in the jasmine-blooming gardens;
bodies still glide in tableau from their darker edges.

Your "hungry soul" laps at the page with its "burning, burning";
your moans send out an echo from their darker edges.

Silk covers your arms, your fingers, your lips, your voice.
Your black lines weave a trousseau from their darker edges.

Wind strikes at the palm trees where you walked;
fronds shake like tousled arrows from their darker edges.

Your nights spread quiet over "parched and dreary" sand.
Finches fill them till they glow from their darker edges.

Lamia To Lycius

"A serpent!" echoed he; no sooner said
than with a frightful scream she vanished
and Lycius' arms were empty of delight,
as were his limbs of life, from that same night.
— John Keats, "Lamia"

Do you hear me, Lycius? Do you hear these dreams
moving like words out of the air, it seems?
You think you saw me thin into a ghost,
impaled by his old eyes, with their shuddering boast
of pride that kills truth with philosophy.
But you hear this voice. It is a serpent's, or
is it a woman's, this rich-emblazoned core
reaching out loud for you, as I once reached
for you with clinging hands, and held you, and beseeched?
I had a woman's tears, and woman's teeth
that could not bite, although the ruddy wreath
of my soft lips was closing. And my heart
crawled like a serpent. And that is the part
you married, Lycius, when you made the sun
shine over my damp earth, and grew with me to one
(I had thought our love was closer than belief,
palpable to outwit such stinging grief).
Now in the empty air, as our mouths grow slow,
open your ears to a voice that will never know
your cold and subtle school's philosophy.
Then speak to me, with your body's memory.

The Intellect of Woman

"The intellect of man is forced to choose
perfection of the life or of the work."
　　　　　　　—Yeats, "The Choice"

The intellect of woman must not choose
perfection of the life, or of the work.
Perfection has a diamond for a muse
who scratches where she only needs to look.

And yet the intellect of woman fears
for imperfection's grandeur, in the sharp
delight that breaks her hearing through her ears,
the edge that cuts her vision through the dark.

So the intellect of woman will not mind
the sight of where the diamond's edge has moved.
Perfection's habit opens us to find
cuts in a window we have never loved.

39

Epithalamium

A Wedding on Earth

That all the woods may answer, and your eccho ring.
— Edmund Spenser

Like the feet that root deep to walk the ground
with circling steps that no one of us can hear,
or the leaves that die just to coil down
through lost blossoms and wait to reappear—
petal, stamen, pistil and fragrant dust
sing with the pollen's trust.
And as each fruit that drips down the earth's strong chin
spills new sugar over an ancient face,
we all hold seeds that vibrate alive within,
and every hardened pod pulls the world's embrace
from a new hiding place.

As oceans, deserts, rivers, and forests move
with the tumbled bodies, sounding hearts,
surfacing eyes and searching wings of love—
and the one and many, whole and parts,
touch to blend, to marry in their own time,
to keep all movings' rhyme—
let your two waiting hearts ring together; bring
sand to emptiness, memory to the full,
home to the night. You hear longest echoes ring
again; you hear how each lunging particle
rocks in a surging lull,

wise and ready, certain to move with love,
salt and sweet and spiralling open worlds,
holding, braided, careful, the voices of
desire and honor. Reach for your unfurled
openness to rock through the earth again, to come,
new and empty, among
every creature. Then keep a steady song,
sounding the ways that marriage, compassion's tool,
rough strong teacher of joy, right-gathering wrong,

oldest puzzle, simple yet tangled rule,
moves, in each molecule.

Marriage is a field where the planet's skin
stretches and wakes open in fertile seeds,
moving patterns through couples. They begin
with shadowed furrows, whose every sowing leads
time-fed opposites, soaked in day and night,
to meet each others' height.
Goddess and god of weddings, help this pair
pair with abundance, to curl wide and alive
with each leaf they send through the long beauty.
Grow them with the depth and the care to strive.
Harvest them, where they thrive.

And as the earth and heat form their crystal sides,
leaping into the shapes listening patterns hold
since the long-gone births of their silent guides
still work minerals into that secret fold,
fanning space, cleaving it with energy
birthed of polarity—
bend them together in fire, and in earth,
willing difference into the ground of change,
mixing powers until a hard new birth,
a tender metamorphosis rearranged,
stays both the same and strange.

Just as in the deepest cold far caves
(the emptiest solid reach of oldest space,
where the stars and solitude grow), black holes
shimmer open thickly with dark to trace
sameness empty, yet fill multitudes the same,
speaking out the never-name,
universes steady and climates clear
at the linking spaces where love exhales.
Breathe again, with such passion you'll pull back near,
voicing closeness down through love's fountained trails,
humming the ancient scales.

Feel yourselves how the bluejay, eagle, swallows,
cardinal, doves and finches, sparrows, terns,
move with long-held wings, find the surge that follows,
dips, fills, rises to pour back up and burns
through warm mornings (or brief songs from trees,
as forests darken to ease—)
how fox, moose, crocodile and koala bear,
elephant, cheetah, deer and cat and squirrel
cry with single breaths until they may pair,
ears and mouths poured open while bodies skirl
towards the enspiralled whirl.

Let your bodies make a body of bodies—cool
with the pores of a question, rich and warm
with answers quickening to beat and roll and spool
through the lost space anchored only by love's vast charm,
where pools of kiss and hope and remembering meet,
crossed in a sculpting heat.
Enter, oh, enter the language of your skins,
where motion mentions silence, and words spill light
over the actual air; let your touch begin
spinning separate souls in one open flight
towards one believed delight.

And you'll reach, with the meanings that humans bid
two more minds to touch from balanced pairs—
intersection of line to pyramid,
uncornered circling, edging angles, squares—
long paradoxes, shaped in geometry's
aisled community.
Goddess and god of weddings, bend your strengths
over your weaving promises and go
past the edges of partnership, through the lengths
of the days that are moving us, fast or slow,
from everything we know.

Marriage is the mirror and crucible
where a true plain face turns to see its own
fullness empty, its emptiness made full
in the shadows that blended love and bone,
half-invisible, burned clear by the light,
cast under mutual sight.
Goddess and god of weddings, press your hearts
wide to reflect the earth, till they touch and share
knowledge, patience, consciousness—human arts—
in wild bodies, and intersperse, and dare
bend in the planet's care.

Now, goddess and god, make marriage. Take your hands
in the sight of these people and the earth,
and one bird finds rest in a valleyed cove,
and more birds take flight in new kinds of birth.
Touch your hands. Touch words. Oh, now turn and
bless
each with that happiness—
your family, earth, friends, guests and the binding day.
Open us with a heart to hear every test,
brave to reach everything we will need to say,
strong to hold our silences, find our rest—
wise, to believe love best.

Two Bodies

Summer Solstice Chant

June 21

The sun, rich and open,
stretches and pours on the bloom of our work.

In the center of the new flowers,
a darker wing of flower

points you like a fire.

Point your fire like a flower.

Paravaledellentine: A Paradelle

For Glen

Come to me with your warning sounds of the tender seas.
Come to me with your warning sounds of the tender seas.
Move me the way the seas' warm sea will spend me.
Move me the way the seas' warm sea will; spend me.
Move your sea-warm come to me; will with me; spend
tender sounds, warning me the way of the seas, the seas.

Tongues sharp as two wind-whipped trees will question.
Tongues sharp as two wind-whipped trees will question.
 (Skin or nerve waiting and heart will answer.
Skin or nerve waiting and heart will answer).
Question will answer two tongues and, or will:
heart sharp as nerve trees; waiting, skin-whipped wind.

Brim your simple hand over where the skin is.
Brim your simple hand over where the skin is.
Wish again, whenever hair and breath come closer.
Wish again, whenever hair and breath come closer.
Closer, again, whenever; brim where your skin is;
hair, wish and breath over the simple hand, come.

Spend come warning me, whenever simple sounds will, will;
move your question. Answer your heart-sharp tender
sea-warm will with me. Way of the seas, the seas!
Where skin-whipped nerve trees wind over waiting tongues,
brim closer to me. Again the skin, as wish,
and two of the breath, hand and hair, or come, is.

Conversation
Edward Weston's "Squash," 1936

"Delve for me, delve down, delve past your body, crowned
by its hidden stem, like a shadowy alarm;
see how you vanish past our dark-shed charm,
throat over throat, ankle to ankle, bound
in our different arches, summer-nicked and browned
interlocking rings in the chain of wrist and arm."

"Lie for me, lie. I want to feel you turn.
Mark out the summer's bending month and learn
to cradle the concrete ground till it softens. Stay.
Measure me past my stem. Though your shadows churn,
close yourself over. Encompass me like clay."

Two Bodies

Two bodies, balanced in mass and power,
move in a bed through the dark,
under the earliest human hour.
A night rocks, like an ark.

They reach through the ceilings of the night,
tall as animals.
Through their valleys bends the light
of their fertile hills.

Two bodies breathe their close hellos
through interlocking pores,
while that hush of beating slows,
held, with many oars,

heart over heart, leg over leg,
trading still breath, until,
heart over heart, and seed into egg,
night holds two bodies still.

A Valentine For Hands

names, silence—quietest minutes
(building like rain or returning like seas)
since they have touched me, your warm hands have sown
gentlest sounds, touches and hours
(or, building like rain, turning, like seas)

(building like rain, or returning like seas)
ripples and springs—the shiniest rivers—
since they have known me your warm hands have gathered
smallest, most stars—happiest skies—
simplest—touched—sounding—hours

The Coming Mirrors

My body thickens in a stem
climbing aloud to keep you here.

My belly thickens like a stem,
my belly is tethered by your days.

Come in, come in, my strong darling.
I'm still a pane of airy glass.

My breasts go heavy to meet you here.

My body turns in place of clouds,
I grow like a pane of open glass.

My body is a forest floor
where needles blend to keep you here.

My belly thickens like a stem.

Come in, come in, my last darling,
and let the coming mirrors pass.

Meeting Mammoth Cave, Eight Months Pregnant

In the night to my humanness
the unparticled has poured,
no beam will sink or angle,
no slow new mineral drip
through the circling ceiling

(loud strength of a darkness
only dark can reassure

(solid cavern's holding,
to hollow the beautiful

carrying dark to hold me,
to empty the slippery

(The loud strength of a darkness
only dark can reassure,

(solid cavern's holding,

No beam will sink or angle,

open cavern's holding,

in the rock to my humanness
unparticled and poured

to hollow the beautiful

(Into no circumference.

Butterfly Lullaby

My wild indigo dusky wing
my mottled, broad-wing skipper,
a sleepy, dreamy dusty wing,
flying through my night.

My northern, southern, cloudy wing,
my spring azure, my crescent pearl,
a silver-spotted, sweet question mark,
sleeping in my sky.

A tiger swallowtail, harvester,
moving through my hours,
an eyed brown in the redwing dark,
wrapped softly in my words.

Belly

"So seems this life on earth, compared with the time that is unknown
to us: as if you sat feasting with your thanes in wintertime, with a
fire burning, and your hall warm, and it rained and snowed and stormed
outside; and a sparrow quickly flew through that house, in through
one of the doors, and out through the other."

           – Bede

Humming sparrow touching my breast
from deep in the dark,

belly turns one voice open in this place of clouds,
turning and tethered by deep in the dark.

Sparrow who is coming, looking for rest,
from deep in the dark,

belly reaps winter open in one flying charm,
tree and belief, heavy fish-rushing spark

of mother and daughter, husband and son,
from deep in the dark,
from deep in the dark.

Over Dark Arches

Naked and thin and wet as if with rain,
bursting I come out of somewhere, bursting again.
And like a great building that breathes under sunlight
over dark arches, your body is there,

And my milk moves under your tongue—

where currents from earth linger under cool stone
rising to me and my mouth makes a circle
over your silence

You reach through your mouth to find me—

Bursting out of your body that held me for years,
as the rain wets the earth with its bodies—

And my thoughts are milk to feed you

till we turn and are empty,

till we turn and are full.

Churching

(The several weeks after childbirth when a woman was
considered unclean and was not allowed to attend church)

Covered with the latitudes of war,
and holding up the blood of my own son

(earth and the water surround you. So I surround you,
leaf over water, stem over stone)

keeping the dark urgency of the long night
I will not go into your church

(scalloped by moons)

I stay here looking at my own blood
(on both sides)
I stay here holding up my blood
(simultaneously)
I will stand here with my own blood
(in adopting forests)

Black and slippery, rusty and strong,
prolific and arching out through my thick hair,
(The hugest, completest old planets are twisting around you)

fervent and striking, aimed at the land
(So you bask alive)

here is my powerblood,

(in the simplest sun)

fruits of my land

my own country

(Reaching through a gate)

This is the blood that came out of the fullness
that grows in me like a forest
(To narrow)
of trees so strong

(or hold)

so much taller than I am
(while spending)

so much dark greener than I am

(to)
Here is this fullness.
(form).

The church is in me, the church of the tall trees.

Earth Goddess and Sky God

Lammas Chant

(two voices, alternating)

Fill the earth's belly full.

Fill the earth's belly full.
Bring the food, bring the grain.
There are cold months ahead
Give them peace in the ground.

Bring the food, bring the grain.

Fill the earth's belly full.
bring the food, bring the grain.
There are cold months ahead.
Give them peace in the ground.

There are cold months ahead.
Give them peace in the ground.

Fill the earth's belly full;
bring the food, bring the grain.
There are cold months ahead.
Give them peace in the ground.

Earth Goddess and Sky God

You haven't formed me. I'm a monster still.

Then give me your body. Give it to me in rain.

Look up and fill me. I am too dark to stain.

You haven't held me. I hold apart my will

Spread dryness through me. I have a night to fill

in high heat-speckled waves, apart from where

I will come down. I have nothing to share

with breath. I will give it back. There is one to kill,

one to renew, and one to persuade to weep.

My night holds everything except for sleep.

Iowa Barn

Light and shadow
frame a window
that comes reaching
past a roof-edge
and becomes a hole. Sky goes
funneling to
any darkness,
cut by warped
wooden framing,
long-abandoned
by the glass that
could reflect us.

Desire For Quiet

Silence may lead deep and make me mad.
If I say "water," it might answer "mud."

The quietness might stop and make me sad,
And kill my carp, my colors' golden blood.

Why should I dig a place for it, here where
The dark is dry grass tipped by brutal flowers?

Hostage Wildflowers

Daisy-grouped hanging sea, wet paintbrush filled
with devil-drops, purple vetch steering its barge,
soaked as long-cold sea-houses, and less tame:

close visitors, the gentle places in grass came
to earth. They trap you wild while the large
rain centers and your drops fall, build, fall, build.

A Dance For The Inland Sea

Water that moves, in a bodylike stream,
through its cool channels fills the warm prairie's dream.
Waking to tend it, the grass-moving sky

pours with grasses. Big Bluestem's drinking roots lie
nine feet down the waving, remembering sod
they have swum through, to feed on, to build. When it swings
like a wing in small flight, when it sways,
turkey feet murmur, red three-toed feet sing.

Little Bluestem, as copper as autumn or clay,
floating seeds past the prairie's dense, watery hand
till they shimmer to columns, wet smoke on the land;

Indian Grass, lapping up the spattering sun;
prairies step slower than palaces, down
under the teeming roof of the ground,
quiet as animals. Then, when they rise,
prairies, like palaces, loom, and surprise.

The August Porch

One afternoon: I think I like it
better for cut browns
apples
lumber

than evening for the ravelling of slats to emerald.

There's no gleam to the wicker.
Shadows might well
not be cast.

The trees are scanty
with the weight
of apples
they have finished.

But wisteria raises
its inchworm head and hunts
for the walls of this porch.

Something's waiting to run out on us.
The mist
and creak
of wines is due
when we run out of dusk.

Wild Yeasts
for Marta

Rumbling a way up my dough's heavy throat to its head,
seeping the trailed, airborne daughters down into the core,
bubbles go rioting through my long-kneaded new bread;
softly, now, breath of the wildest yeast starts to roar.
My hands work the peaked foam, push insides out into the light,
edge shining new sinews back under the generous arch
that time's final sigh will conclude. (Dry time will stretch tight
whistling stops of quick heat through my long-darkened starch.)

How could I send quiet through this resonant, strange, vaulting roof
murmuring, sounding with spores and the long-simple air,
and the bright free road moving? I sing as I terrace a loaf
out of my hands it has filled like a long-answered prayer.
Now the worshipping savage cathedral our mouths make will lace
death and its food, in the moment that refracts this place.

Calendar of approximate years in which these poems were completed or substantially completed:

1970 Caribou Kitchen
1978 The August Porch
1985 Blue Willows
1985 Desire for Quiet
1986 Hostage Wildflowers
1986 To My Unborn
1987, 2000 The Woman on the Beach
1987, 2000 Earth Goddess to Sky God
1988 Moon
1989 Interpenetrate
1989 The Menstrual Hut
1989, 2000 To Vivienne Eliot
1990 The Intellect of Woman
1990, 2000 Churching
1990, 2000 Belly
1993 Letter for Emily Dickinson
1994 Lamia to Lycius
1995 Faces With Poulenc
1995 Landing Under Water, I See Roots
1995 A Seed for Spring Equinox
1995 Imbolc Chant
1995 Lammas Chant
1995 Summer Solstice Chant
1995 Winter Solstice Chant

1996 A Dance for the Inland Sea
1996 Iowa Barn
1996 Mowing
1996, 2000 Wild Yeasts
1997 Boothbay Harbor
1997 Elegy for My Father
1997 Final Autumn
1997 Name
1997 The Coming Mirrors
1998 Butterfly Lullaby
1998 Over Dark Arches
1998 Two Bodies
1998 Without a Bird
1998, 2002 Meeting Mammoth Cave,
     Eight Months Pregnant
1999 Ghazal for a Poetess
1999 A Valentine for Hands
1999 A Wedding on Earth
1999 Chain of Women
2000 A Carol for Carolyn
2000 Calendars
2000 Conversation
2000 Paravaledellentine: A Paradelle
2000 Watching the Oregon Whale